On the Edge of Knowing

On the Edge of Knowing

Poems by

Sam Aureli

© 2026 Sam Aureli. All rights reserved.
This material may not be reproduced in any form, published,
reprinted, recorded, performed, broadcast,
rewritten or redistributed without
the explicit permission of Sam Aureli.
All such actions are strictly prohibited by law.

Cover design by Shay Culligan
Cover image by Joshua Earle
Chapter images from Unsplash
Author photo by Sam Aureli

ISBN: 979-8-90146-603-2

Kelsay Books
502 South 1040 East, A-119
American Fork, Utah 84003
Kelsaybooks.com

For Mom.

*Your spirit shaped my voice,
your love grounded my roots.*

More Praise for On the Edge of Knowing

A fine collection. Transporting, descriptive, and at times ethereal. It is equal parts observations of nature through an inquisitive lens, a call to go outside and feel for yourself the synergies in our nexus with the natural world. *On the Edge of Knowing* is a moving collection. You'll feel many a final line like a thud in your center.
 —Bri Bruce, Author and Editor-in-Chief, *Humana Obscura*

Aureli's collection invites us into his heart and mind to pause at wonder. He shows us an innocence and respect to how he sees the world.

This collection makes you stand still and be in the moment with Aureli looking at the world through curious eyes. His use of language is brilliantly haunting, depicting just how alive the earth is. Ultimately, Aureli's poems do what poems do best—leaving us appreciative and questioning of our place in this world and the strength of nature.
 —Charlotte Cosgrove, Poet and Editor, *Rough Diamond Poetry*

On the Edge of Knowing, in which Sam presents a luminous collection of poems that meditate on impermanence, belonging, and the quiet intelligence of the natural world.

With lyrical precision and deep sensitivity, Aureli traces the shifting landscapes of memory, grief, and wonder. From starlit skies to tidal shores, the poems penned in this collection are intimate and expansive, inviting you into stillness, reflection, and the beauty of what cannot be fully grasped—the enigma. It is a stirring debut that listens closely to the world and the silence that resides in it.
 —Arzu Deniz, Editor-in-Chief, *Prosetrics the Magazine*

There is something elemental in Sam Aureli's poetic interpretation of nature; he offers us a flawless mirror on the world he sees about him, and invites us to be as moved by it as he is—"drifting where the current calls, wholly this, and nothing less."

—Ian Gouge, Author, *17 Alma Road*

This richly evocative poetry collection takes on mankind's relationship with Nature, but not in the usual way. The poet doesn't approach Nature as merely a force, a thing, an *Other,* but as a *Who.*

This collection is very much the study of a relationship, gradual and mysterious, yet deeply familiar, the kind that springs up between strangers. From fleeting glances to gaining trust, there's a deepening of dialogue and kinship that evolves both through the seasons—and through the poet's lifetime.

As with any true friendship, it takes time, discovering similarities, accepting differences, gaining courage and unlikely inspiration, changing one another bit by bit—until a resemblance takes root, not just in the day-to-day but in the soul.

"Leaning in to listen" is a repeated motif and a departure from the usual "observer and observed" approach. It is a meditation on the ways in which we seek to know Nature, but also acknowledging Nature as a *someone* who also seeks to know us in return.

Aureli blends both majesty and intimacy, weaving contemplation with soul-knowing, to portray an ever-deepening bond with Nature, both revealing and reveling in the overlapping of heartbeats—flesh and blood and cosmic.

—Hanna Nielson, Editor-in-Chief, *The Belfast Review*

Acknowledgments

This chapbook is dedicated to my mother, Anna Cavaricci. Her unwavering encouragement, her constant push to explore the depths of my craft, and her enduring reminder to stay rooted in where I come from have profoundly shaped who I am, both as a person and a poet. She passed away on January 11, 2024, but her presence continues to guide me.

I am deeply grateful to my family and friends, who have walked beside me on this journey. Their love, support, and belief in me have been my greatest strength.

I extend heartfelt appreciation to those who supported the development of this collection. Whether through reviewing the manuscript, offering thoughtful feedback, or lending their generous endorsement, your contributions have meant the world to me.

In particular, I'd like to thank Hanna Nielson for her thoughtful guidance throughout the editing process. She spent a generous amount of time offering insightful feedback and helped me make sense of the collection when I needed it most. Her support was invaluable.

I'm also grateful to Chrissy Swisher, Ellen Rowland, Jeff Bogle, Asheley Nova Navarro, Ian Gouge, Bri Bruce, Charlotte Cosgrove, and Arzu Deniz for taking the time to review the manuscript and for their encouragement, insights, and belief in this work. Your feedback made a real difference.

My sincere thanks also go to the editors of the following journals and magazines where several of these poems first appeared, sometimes in slightly different form:

The Atlanta Review: "Lost in the Woods"
Coverstory Books: "On the Edge of Knowing"
Crow & Cross Keys: "Walking Past the End"
Everscribe Magazine: "Blueberries for All," "Why We Keep Going"
Humana Obscura: "Drifting Ochre," "On Living," "Hinoki and Cedarwood"
Loft Books: "The Last Leaf"
Moss Puppy Magazine: "Beneath the Old Oak"
Prosetrics, The Literary Magazine: "Even Now, the Light," "In the Waiting"
Ragaire Literary Magazine: "Don't Rush Growing"
Rough Diamond Poetry: "A Dialogue of Earth and Sky," "Song of Belonging," "Call It Soul"
Sidhe Press: "Elegy for a Hawthorn"
Sontag Mag: "Navigating the Night," "A Morning's Apology"
Stanchion Magazine: "The Indifference of Snow"

Special thanks as well to the photographers whose images are featured in the collection. Their work adds another dimension of meaning and resonance to these poems. Photo credits are as follows:

Tree: Johannes Kopf
Poppies: Sies Kranen, "Poppies Everywhere"
Driftwood: Joshua Profitt

Each image is used with permission through the Unsplash license, and I remain grateful for the opportunity to include their artistry alongside my words.

Contents

PART ONE

Between Stars and Silence	15
Speck of Dust	16
The Stars Bear Witness	17
Ribbons of Light	18
Salt and Sway	19
Hinoki and Cedarwood	20
A Dialogue of Earth and Sky	21
The Quiet Work of Growing	22
Crocus	23
Magnolias Do Not Hesitate	24
In the Waiting	25
Green Promise	26
Blueberries for All	27
Song of Belonging	28

PART TWO

Petals Hold Their Tongues	33
Veiled Dawn	34
Beneath the Old Oak	36
The Stillness Between	37
Lost in the Woods	38
Navigating the Night	40
Cedar in the Storm	41
Walking Past the End	42
Forsythia	43
Drifting Ochre	44
The Last Leaf	45
Some Last Sweetness	46

Whisper at the Edge	47
Even Now, the Light	48
Shouldering What We Can	50
Poppies Don't Mind	51

PART THREE

Skimming Over Prairie Grass	57
Don't Rush Growing	58
Elegy for a Hawthorn	59
Echoes After Dust	60
The Great, Unwritten Dark	61
To Die Is to Live Again	62
Against a Fevered Night	63
Call It Soul	64
Wind in the Wheat	66
All That I Am	68
Why We Keep Going	70
The Indifference of Snow	72
A Morning's Apology	73
Church of Roots and Stone	74
On Living	76
On the Edge of Knowing	77

NOTES	83

PART ONE

*We are what the stars are made of.
We are of the dust of the earth, and the dust of the stars,
and we carry the songs of the universe in our bones.*

—N. Scott Momaday

Between Stars and Silence

The earth turns,
a blue pearl in the void,
poised between fire and ice.

Spinning just so.
A fraction off, and breath would fade,
tides might shrug the moon's pull,
and we'd drift, cut loose in the dark.

Yet oceans brush the shore,
waves rising and falling,
a blind hand tracing
the curve of a familiar face.

Was it whispered into being,
a sigh from ancient depths,
or flung here,
a coin cast into a cosmic well?

And me?
I'm just a bit of motion,
a pocket of warm blood,
caught midway through the mystery,
turning it over,
a dull penny found
on a street I don't remember walking.

Speck of Dust

Weightless, afloat in a golden drift,
I wander the shadowed cosmos.
What spirit stirs this flickering breath,
this shimmer I dare call my own?
I reach for a thread of fire,
a glow to cleave the haze,
still stumbling through the night.

The Stars Bear Witness

And what of the night,
that vast, dark river,
whispers older than memory
beneath a weave of stars?

We walk its ancient edge,
our breath sharp as frost,
silence deep as bone.
Still, the path unfolds.

Above, the Great Bear burns,
kindled by eternal fire.
It holds our gaze,
asks only that we listen.

And what do you hear
when the trail fades past
the rim of the world,
when the weary plead for dawn?

Come close to the flame.
Its voice, earth-deep,
crackles with the tongue
of those who named the skies.

Ribbons of Light

The sky unspools a rapid ribbon,
pink as cotton candy, or a dream
half-remembered. I lift my hands
to catch it, frame it, but let it slip.
How does the sun choose its shades?
The light frays soft, and I'm left
tracing what fades too fast to hold.
Some answers belong to the dark,
unfolding where the ribbon rests.

Salt and Sway

I stand alone in the Cape's
rippling waters:

my feet shift—
coarse sands, broken shells,
pebbles pressing my tender soles.

Waves rise and pass,
lapping at my chest,
softly folding onto the shore.

The sun scatters
across the crests, each glint
a brief gift in the tide's steady breath.

Above, piping plovers
trace the horizon, small, pale wings drawn
by a pulse I trust, but do not know.

Here, I let go,
surrender to the salt and sway,
drifting where the current calls,
wholly this, and nothing less.

Hinoki and Cedarwood

Walk softly through the valley,
among the tender green of woods.
Pause—let the world exhale.
Draw in the sharp, resinous air,
hinoki rising like a memory,
rain murmuring its soft hymn,
brushing leaf, pattering earth.
Listen—branches sway,
cedar whispers a song that rises
and falls with your breath.
Hold this. Let it etch its weight
into your chest, settle
like water on stone.
Beneath this patient pulse,
what I carry softens.

A Dialogue of Earth and Sky

The rain drums its fingers
on the canvas roof,
traces silver veins
along the canopy's edge,
whispers gossip to the ivy geranium,
which nods in its sleep.

A hummingbird,
late for an appointment,
hovers—vanishes.

The thick heat of summer
lifts its face.
I name it *petrichor,*
but the rain already knows.

Barefoot now,
I step out,
let the water
write its name on me.

The Quiet Work of Growing

An Ode to the Sunflower

Beneath winter's weight,
a quiet prayer rests in the dark,
folded deep, spared from frost.

Then, the thaw—
something stirs beneath the silence.
A green thread breaks the stubborn earth,
reaching for the sky.

Florets blaze, like stars in the field,
lifting golden faces to the sun.
They linger in that high, unshadowed hour,
cradled in the shimmer of noon's boundless breath.

Soon, crowns heavy with light bow,
petals loosening, drifting like breath,
seed by seed returning.

Did it not dazzle the sky,
sing of light,
teach the weary earth hope?

And we—brief, radiant—
might still bloom.

Crocus

Sunlight slips past the curtain,
presses warm against my face,
searching for signs of life.
I blink, exhale, something
like steam rises from my chest.

Outside, the trees are listening.
A robin plucks a song
from the wind's pocket,
scatters it like crumbs on the cold earth.
Little ghosts of winter watch from the shadows.

I run my hand over dampened leaves,
as if searching for a pulse.
A crocus, pale and trembling,
pushes up like a forgotten word,
a murmur of spring's old promise.

I wait, unmoving.
It speaks first.

Magnolias Do Not Hesitate

Spring unfurls its wings
shaking off the last shiver of frost.
A tender promise unfolds,

petals yawning open to the light.
The air hums with bees and birdsong,
earth-drunk on its own renewal.

But already, my thoughts slip ahead—
summer's fire crackles; autumn leans in,
brushes dipped in gold and cooling ember.

And winter—vast winter—
lurking at the edges, patient, unblinking.
Still, warm winds carry the scent of blossoms,

and the magnolias do not hesitate.

In the Waiting

I kneel in the asparagus patch,
shears in hand,
cutting back the brittle ghosts
of last year's growth,
each stem a memory,
each snip, a quiet prayer.

The earth does not flinch.
It takes the gesture
without question.

Nothing breaks the surface yet,
but I ready the soil anyway,
my hands learning
the slow language of return.

This, too, is how we live:
clearing what no longer blooms,
trusting the root
that waits in silence
to rise.

Green Promise

In the backyard,
a hawthorn leans into the wind,
an offering of white flowers
and red berries.

It stood long before me,
rooted in ovum-silence.

One night, a storm came,
split it in two.
For a season, it grieved.

Spring arrived.
The forsythia burned yellow,
but the hawthorn held its silence,
blossoms curled into memory.

Then—
a single sprig,
small hands reaching
for the sun.

Blueberries for All

I give thanks for the rows
of blueberry shrubs, tall as old men
nodding beside the shed,
remnants of a farm
long folded into memory.

Every morning, turkeys strut in—
heads bowed, then leaping,
wings awkward,
snatching at the highest fruit.
Jays and robins flit behind,
sharp-eyed, quick-clawed.

People ask how I keep them away.
As if I would. I let them eat.
By tomorrow, the bushes bow again,
laden with what the land offers freely.

The wild things take what they need.
I stand in their shadows,
palms open,
watching.

Song of Belonging

My feet find earth,
sink into its dark, unbroken humus.
The sycamore speaks,
its tendons taut against the pull of time,
bones of my being entangled
with roots older than names.
Each mile unfurls, a thread of earthen song,
weaving me back to the first horizon,
to the birthplace of my shadow.

PART TWO

Let me keep my mind on what matters,
which is my work, which is mostly standing still
and learning to be astonished.

—Mary Oliver

Petals Hold Their Tongues

Flowers hum at a pitch
only the faithful can hear.
To the uninvited,
they turn bitter,
close their veins,
hold their tongues.

A bee arrives.
Their sweetness quickens.

How wise they are,
knowing when to open,
when to wither—
their roots steady beneath
the wild turn of seasons.

And here I stand,
shaped by the same earth,
the same relentless refrain—

perhaps it lingers,
nesting beneath the clamor,
waiting for silence
to hum in return.

Veiled Dawn

Obscurity blankets the backyard,
barely a glimpse beyond the shed.
Blueberry shrubs drown in mist.

This is only a momentary veil.
I know what lies beyond:
I've walked these woods,
felt the bark of the eastern white pines,
their resin clinging to my palms
like a promise I meant to keep.

But now, my hands
hang like dead branches.
Doubt creeps in,
its shadow feeding on pause.

A doe steps from beyond,
breath clouding the air,
as if the world were always hers.
The grass glows greener
where she treads.

I could stay,
a shadow among shadows,
or I could walk,
feet pressing into silence,
toward whatever calls my name.

Beneath the Old Oak

We played beneath the old oak,
the one that held the sky,
its roots sinking deep into the earth.
Our laughter soared with the swing,
always reaching, never touching.

But time, a slow tide,
pulled us apart.
Duty came, and the swing's creak
softened to silence,
rusted chains unraveling.

Regret sang a steady tune,
and the distance grew,
quiet, aching.

Now the swing is still,
an old tire buried in mud,
a whisper left to the wind.

The Stillness Between

The seasons hesitate,
a white sheet pulled tight,
rain tapping riddles on the roof.

No answer. Only stillness,
time unraveling in threads
of frost and flame.

The cat, that old conspirator,
paces the threshold,
weighing the brittle cold against
the comfort of a cozy fire.

Caught between choices—
do I bow to the frost,
let sorrow root like ice,
or turn toward the ember buried deep,
a flicker I could cradle from the wind?

Lost in the Woods

The great American beech looms,
its autumn leaves scattered below,
scaly cones of the eastern white pines lie
spent among broken twigs.
The crunch beneath my feet fills the quiet.

No one travels here but the deer,
the squirrel, the wood thrush singing.
Fresh scrapes mark the fissured tulip bark,
a black bear speaking in a tongue
only the wild remembers.
My claws are mute,
my voice without melody.

The wind carries the forest chatter—
creaking branches, tumbling leaves.
The aging white birch, skin unfolding,
leans close and whispers,
Where are you going?

I've roamed poplars and spruces,
brushed the stag's graze,
heard the mourning dove coo,
sought the great horned owl by night,
yet these woods grow strange to me.

In the distance, a brook's rush
threads through roots and worn stone,
its babble a steady hand
guiding me toward open waters,
where the silt of the world drifts on.

Navigating the Night

Another moonless night
in Franconia, the distant glow
beyond the horizon lost to me.
I wonder if the black bear,
earlier roaming fields
of wildflowers, prowls now, seeking
a midnight feast. No poppies
bloom tonight.

Then—a flicker of light,
and another. One by one,
they begin their ballet, tiny fires,
lightning bugs in countless
throngs. Guided by some quiet
purpose, they drift as if born to pierce
this harrowing dark.

Cedar in the Storm

I peel away, cedar planks split,
nails loosened by the gnaw of rain,
a husk left to the mercy of the wind.

How long—this rattling, this creak,
a door unlatched in the storm? I wait
for silence to settle. The night mutters its

riddles—jagged whispers of doubt,
answers slipping through my fingers,
thin as unraveling thread.

I cling to the frame of myself,
braced against the night,
listening for the calm of dawn.

Walking Past the End

The vultures tilt in a slow gyre overhead,
black commas punctuating
a sentence I don't yet know the end of.
Their shadows stitch the dirt at my feet,
a clock with no hands, tightening.

I wonder if it's my name
scratched into their hunger,
or if some other luckless thing
has caught their eye—a deer, a dog,
a stranger who paused too long.

I keep walking, heels grinding dust,
pretending the air isn't thickening,
that the squawks aren't a chorus rehearsing
my exit. A stick snaps underfoot.
I tell myself it's nothing.
Just the world, practicing.

Forsythia

It's not the tulip or the daffodil
that marks the change for me,
nor the crocus
cracking the earth
by the stone wall.

Snow recedes,
revealing what storms forgot—
a glove, a toy,
a rusted nail still clinging.

I look back.
Some losses fresh,
some just outlines now.
Will this year be different?
I've stopped asking.

Today, driving home
from nowhere in particular,
I saw the forsythia—
bright, burning yellow
at the field's edge,
not waiting, just there.

Drifting Ochre

A single leaf of yellow ochre
floats along the water's gentle current.
It spins and twirls, as if remembering
all it had known—the warmth of spring,
the quiet labor of becoming,
a life steeped in sun and rain.

The stream nudges it forward,
over rocks and eddies, past roots
and shadows, urging it on
along a path unasked, untraced.
The leaf didn't need to know.
There was only
the freedom of letting go.

And as I watched, I thought:
all things drift in time,
each in our own rivers and bends,
our passage carved by wind and water,
until the earth calls us back,
her soil rich
with all that has come before.

The Last Leaf

I am the last leaf,
clinging to the sturdy oak
whose roots grip the earth.

The wind pulls at me, whispering
through my edges,
as branches bend and creak.
I hold, trembling.

Around me, the air bites colder,
leaves rustle their final descent,
the sky deepens to dusk.
I remain,
witness to a season slipping away,
as if my frail grip
could halt the fading light.

Soon, I will let go.
But not yet.

Some Last Sweetness

Do you ever feel it—
your life, withered, softly rattling,
like the spindly arms of a December tree,

a few leaves still clinging,
held by a thread,
not yet ready to release,

as if some last sweetness might
stir within them, while the wind
moves through the bare dusk?

Whisper at the Edge

An Ode to the Lichen Cladonia Cristatella

Rockabema Lake holds its breath,
a mirror of sky and tree,
stillness pressing gently on my chest.

I sit on the weathered dock,
feet above the hush,
silence threading through my fingers.

Between the cracks, a tiny red flower unfolds,
a whisper of fire on old cedar,
velvet crowns warm with life.

It says nothing,
expects nothing,
but here I am, leaning in.

Even Now, the Light

Listen—
the earth still breathes beneath our hurried steps,
its ancient pulse dwelling in the roots of trees,
in the hush between waves.

But we do not hear it.
We walk with our heads bent,
hands full of loss,
as night folds itself over the fields,
as the wind threads through the reeds.
Even the moon turns away.

But not all is lost.

Look—
how morning spills light
into the empty spaces,
how the hermit thrush lifts
a note of gold against the fading dark.

Spring comes anyway.

And what is the sun,
if not the hand of mercy?
What is the woodland song,
if not a voice calling us home?

Even now, the earth begins again.
Even now, there is light enough
to find our way.

Shouldering What We Can

I can't carry your burden—
not for lack of love,
but because I wake each morning
beneath the weight of my own.

We move through this scorched world,
each of us bearing
more than we ever imagined.

But I can walk beside you,
and listen.
Let your sorrow rise
like morning mist,
my quiet presence
something steady to lean on.

It won't lift the weight,
not really.

But for a while,
you might feel less alone,
forget how heavy it's been,
just long enough
to breathe again.

Poppies Don't Mind

I settle on the back porch,
watching the deep orange globe
smear its yawn across the rippled horizon.

With guitar cradled close,
my fingers coax *Dandelion Wine*—
a halting stutter of notes.

The red poppies I nurtured last fall
flare into bloom,
snagging my gaze as they tilt
and shiver in the gentle breeze,
dancing to their mute refrain.
Their ease makes my chest hum.

A note splinters,
then another trips off the fretboard.
The poppies, bless them, sway on
deaf to my sour chords,
but I flinch, the missteps gnawing.
I learned early to chew on flaws.
Still, I pluck on,
because it's how life plays:

I stumble, falter,
stack regrets like jagged shale,
missed shots cutting through the grain,
yet I keep on keeping on,
denying the bent notes
the final say in my tune.

PART THREE

*I have seen sparks fly out
when two stones are rubbed,
so perhaps it is not dark inside after all.*

—Charles Simic

Skimming Over Prairie Grass

Not all roads rise from the same soil.
Some drift like mist from the valley's cradle,
veiled by cedar and willow.
Others claw free from mountain stone,
scored by wind and ice.
Yet they converge, as rivers do,
flowing toward the vast, unknowable sea.

My steps ripple through the current,
jagged with memory's edge,
heavy with untold truths.

Still, the path unwinds,
and I see: we are visitors here,
brief as the ember before ash,
transient as the hawk's shadow
skimming prairie grass.
Yet, meaning burns—
a star blazing on the horizon,
beckoning us onward.

Chase the spark that stirs your hunger,
the flame that maps the night.
Follow it through bramble and stone,
until the road falls silent,
and the sky gathers you in.

Don't Rush Growing

I watch pollen drift in the morning light,
flecks of promise
swayed by the whim of wind.

Their path unseen,
they drift as if aimless,
wandering the open air,
untethered, unclaimed.

But maybe this is
their last taste of freedom
before the earth's gentle take,
its quiet pull toward soil.

And though it lingers—
a season, sometimes more—
purpose will unfold:
in root,
in bloom,
in the quiet insistence
of new life.

Elegy for a Hawthorn

In the first, pale light of spring,
I stand before the hawthorn—
once a keeper of the season's turning,
now bowed low with winter's weight.

The lawn glistens with dew.
Buds, small and green, begin to open—
one last sleight of hand. I hold the saw
and hesitate.

A wood thrush lands lightly
on a crooked branch. Its song
a small lantern.

The tree listens. I listen.

Somewhere beneath us, roots
go on whispering,
making their slow, dark arguments
against time.

Echoes After Dust

Nobody knows what's waiting
for us after the sun sinks, when we trip
into the dark. There may be no reckoning
of deeds, no ink-stained clerk to tally
what we owe. A river with
no questions, just a current chewing
on stones. Yet one day, after tracing
the warped grain of memory's wood,
when your body creaks
and your heart aches, you'll rest
in the only comfort left, asking yourself
if the years were enough to forgive.
And in that silence, as you measure time
by the ghosts it left behind,
what will you say?

The Great, Unwritten Dark

Look how my breath rises,
a small fog in the cold air,
gathering itself into little lives
of water slipping away.
I watch it vanish,
and think of how we, too, go—
the doings of our hands,
the trodden earth,
laughter breaking silence—
all of it softening,
like dusk-born mist,
when the wild breath of the world
lifts us,
piece by tender piece,
into whatever comes after.

To Die Is to Live Again

One day, I will go gently,
crossing into the shadowed woods,
the stars my only lanterns,
their faint gleam tracing what fades.

When this body softens into earth,
let it return as it must—
to soil, to seed, to root.
Scatter me where the wind hums,
where the fields, bright with wildflowers,
will remember my name.

And if you walk there,
let the petals brush your hands.
Perhaps you will feel
how the earth still holds me,
how I bloom again,
small but steadfast,
among the living.

Against a Fevered Night

Does the pale goddess,
in all her fullness,
ever feel the pull of envy,
as she gazes down upon green forests,
beaches the color of sifted gold,
oceans a wide, shifting blue?

There she dangles,
alone in the dark,
watching fires flicker
beyond her silver reach,
keeping our world steady,
waters in motion,
guiding birds along unseen paths.

And yet, never a word of complaint—
just her soft return each night,
a mother placing a cool cloth
against a fevered night.

Call It Soul

> *Whatever this is that I am, it is flesh*
> *and a little spirit and an intelligence.*
> —Marcus Aurelius

I watch my hand in the half-light—
a weathered map of old roads,
dusty towns, and forgotten rivers.
Scars like cryptic inscriptions,
creases where shadows settle.

It moves without asking,
writes its own story,
pulls the past from my pockets,
cups water, cups air, cups silence.

I am a collection of moving parts,
bone and sinew,
a murmuring machine,
thought leaping between circuits
like a bird too restless to land.

Somewhere in this tangle of wires,
something flickers—
a small and stubborn flame.
Not the hand, not the mind,
but the thing neither can touch.

Call it soul, call it ghost.
It waits in the dim,
watching the eye watching it.

Wind in the Wheat

Ekphrastic inspired by Wheat Field with Cypresses by Vincent van Gogh

I stood among something holy,
where wheat leans like a prayer
beneath a sky swirling with thought.

The cypress speaks in shadows,
not loud, but certain,
a bridge between earth and sky.
Olive trees murmur
stories just beyond reach.

Clouds curl like brushstrokes
from a half-woken dream,
the edge trembling
as though the world, too,
is on the verge of remembering.

At the field's end,
where gold gives way
to silver-green,
poppies linger—
not many, just enough to recall
something once said,
and quietly forgotten.

This is not a storm,
but a stirring.
Someone once saw the world tremble
and called it beautiful.

All That I Am

Something stirs,
slipping through roots,
a shadow bending the grass.
An unseen hand rearranges the dust,
loosening names long buried.

I feel it—
a breath at the back of my neck,
a pulse in the marrow of stone.
The trees lean in, listening.
A river dreams beneath its frozen skin.

This is the language of the old ones:
a hush spun into wind,
watching, remembering.

I am only a pilgrim,
fumbling with small words,
turning them over
like bones worn down by silence.

The earth waits,
unraveling time in the curl of a leaf,
in the slow breath of moss,
in the vanishing of my name.

Why We Keep Going

Because the robin keeps singing
even after the branch
has bent beneath her.

Because a poem
can be a steady hand on the back
when no one else stays.

Because grief does not knock,
and neither do we.
We just arrive
with whatever language we have left.

I write
not to be heard by thousands
but to find the one
standing barefoot in a dim kitchen,
cup cooling in her hand,
reading by the light
of what I almost didn't say.

Because silence is heavier
than the weight of being misunderstood.

Because sometimes,
a poem is the only place
where truth doesn't tremble.

You ask, why bother.
I ask—what else is there
that even briefly
makes the heart
recognize itself?

The Indifference of Snow

I cannot tell if the birds are thankful,
if they sense who tends to their hunger—
breaking the snow's silence with a shovel,
scattering seeds on gentler ground,
beyond the ordered offering of the feeder.

Does it matter if they know?
Would their blindness to my gift
reshape the curve of my hand,
diminish the sweep of my will?
They are creatures of instinct,
drawn to the bare, stark truth of survival.

The snow falls still,
indifferent,
answering nothing.

And yet—
my hand returns to the seed,
my heart to the quiet work of giving.

A Morning's Apology

The backyard is a soft white plain,
snow laid down in perfect silence,
sparkling as though someone had shattered
the stars, scattering them carelessly

across the world. The sky, shoulders
unburdened, leans down tenderly, an apology
in the language of light. And the sun tosses
handfuls of brilliance as if to say: look, look

what remains. The northern cardinal begins
a gentle song, threading its music through
the quiet. The air, still and calm, holds
the weight of what was and the promise

of what will be. And I stand here,
listening,
as though peace had always lived
just on the other side of this dark.

Church of Roots and Stone

The sun spills through the canopy,
light tracing the old bones of maples,
beeches standing like sentries.
Leaves rustle secrets,
a chickadee pins a note to the air,
and I walk on,
not yet knowing what I seek,
but drawn forward all the same.

I carry no offerings,
just the ache of asking.

The brook chants a cold prayer,
too weary to quarrel with the world.
It slips past birches,
their bark peeling like forgotten letters—
pale and thin,
roots cradling a stillness
we've long let slip away.

I kneel in their shadow,
bone and breath stilled,
as if the ground remembers
what I've forgotten.
No words.
Just silence, heavier than a sermon.

Pine resin drifts—
breath sharper than air,
older than thought.

Here, in this church of roots and stone,
the trees do not preach.
They do not ask for belief.
They mend.
They whisper, *you are already whole.*

On Living

Not the summit, but the slope—
the grit underfoot, where ferns clutch crevices,
their small green gestures of patience.

I stop where a rock wobbles,
let my breath find the pace of trees,
the silent, unhurried life of moss.

Here, each step unspools its own weight,
not chasing, not held by anything more
than the next steady press of earth.

On the Edge of Knowing

There is a moment, a cusp when the sum of gathered experience is worn down by the details of living. We are never so wise as when we live in this moment.
—Paul Kalanithi

Suddenly, I know what I want—
to be scattered by the sea,
where waves churn sand into bone,
and wind stirs my ash with driftwood.

I have no use for the frail
certainties of man, or for those who sit
with their stories clutched tight,
as if time could still be held.

What I want is this—
to lose myself among the details:
the salt on my skin,
the gull's cry that shatters silence,
the tide's slow pull,
the way the sun bends low at dusk,
its light thinning, then gone.

For there is a moment,
when all I have gathered
crumbles like sand,

and I,
for once,
am wise enough
to let it be.

*To listen deeply
is to live again.*

NOTES

The quote attributed in Part One to N. Scott Momaday, reportedly from the 1997 interview *Conversations with N. Scott Momaday,* has no verifiable source in his published interviews or writings. My research suggests that this line may be an embellishment or paraphrase inspired by Carl Sagan's famous 1973 statement from *The Cosmic Connection:* "We are made of star-stuff."

The quote attributed in Part Two to Mary Oliver, originates from her poem *Messenger,* the opening piece in her 2006 collection *Thirst* (Beacon Press, 2006).

The quote attributed in Part Three to Charles Simic, originates from his poem *Stone*, which can be found in his poetry collection titled *What the Grass Says* (Kayak Press, 1967).

Poppies Don't Mind: The song *Dandelion Wine* is the first track on Gregory Alan Isakov's album *This Empty Northern Hemisphere.* He is one of my all-time favorite musical artists, with a voice as sweet as honey.

Call It Soul: The quote attributed to Marcus Aurelius at the beginning of the poem comes from *Meditations* (Modern Library, 2003), written during his campaign near the River Gran among the Quadi. In the context of the poem, the quote sets the tone for a deeper look at the question: what is the soul, really? It invites us to think about what part of us endures, matters, or makes us who we are.

There's a personal twist to this, too. According to some extensive research by my Zio Silvano, our family tree supposedly traces all the way back to Marcus Aurelius himself. He even collaborated on a book with Luciano Pelliccioni di Poli, titled *I Conti Aureli di Poggio Aquilone* (Self-Published). It's an intriguing idea, though I admit I'm skeptical about how verifiable any of it really is. Still, it adds a strange, almost mythic layer to thinking about legacy, identity, and what we pass down—whether through blood or thought.

On the Edge of Knowing: The quote attributed to Paul Kalanithi at the beginning of the poem comes from his book, *When Breath Becomes Air* (Random House, 2016). This poem emerged after listening to the audiobook, his words striking a quiet chord. There was something about hearing them spoken aloud—gently, plainly—that made them settle deeper.

It got me thinking about my own mortality, not in a dramatic way, but in that quiet, sobering way that makes you stop and really consider how you're spending the time you've been given. That moment he describes—the cusp between what we've learned and what we're living—it felt familiar. I realized I often live at that edge, trying to hold everything together, when maybe the real wisdom is in letting some of it go.

This poem, like the rest of the collection, is an attempt to do just that—to let go, to pay attention, and to be present enough to notice the small, fleeting moments that shape a life.

About the Author

Sam Aureli, originally from Italy and now based in the Boston area, is a design and construction professional working in real estate development. When he's not immersed in concrete and steel, he writes poetry rooted in the elemental textures of the world—cedarwood, tides, ochre leaves. He came to poetry later in life as a refuge from the noise, a way to pause and listen more closely to what the world quietly offers: the wisdom in birdsong, the lessons folded into seasons, the stillness between moments.

His poems have appeared, or are forthcoming, in *The Berlin Review, The Poetry Lighthouse, Amethyst Review, Bloomin' Onion, Bournemouth Journal, Funicular Magazine, Three Panels Press, Underscore Magazine, Dolomite Review, Turning Leaf Journal, Door Is a Jar, Chestnut Review, Moss Puppy Magazine, Bainbridge Island Press,* among other journals. Sam was also the Grand Prize Winner in *The October Project*'s 2025 Poetry Contest, as well as a finalist in the *Good Life Poetry* HoneyBee Prize.

Website: samaureli.com
X/Twitter: @SamthePoet0731
Facebook: @sam.aureli
Instagram: @samaurelipoet
Substack: samaureli.substack.com

www.ingramcontent.com/pod-product-compliance
Lightning Source LLC
Chambersburg PA
CBHW071121160426
43196CB00013B/2665